Secret Agent
Finn McMissile

𝒟ısɴᴇʏ PRESS
New York • Los Angeles

Finn is a secret agent.
Where is Finn?

Here is Finn.
He is hiding.

Here is Finn.
He is swimming.

Here is Finn.
He is climbing.

Here is Finn.
He is flying.

Here is Finn.
He is kicking.

Here is Finn.
He is special!

CONTENTS

Technology advanced rapidly during the late nineteenth and early twentieth centuries. The invention of technologies such as the telephone and radio dazzled people. Practical ways of generating and distributing electricity brought improved lights to city streets and even to some homes. Gasoline and diesel engines made automobiles possible, giving people the ability to move overland quickly without relying on railroads.

These rapid changes inspired some people to dream of a time when mechanical devices would take on difficult, dangerous, and unpleasant jobs. Some imagined mechanical human beings would move in the same way as real people, but they wouldn't tire or get hurt.

In 1920, the author Karel Čapek wrote a play called *R.U.R.* The title was an abbreviation for *Rossum's Universal Robots.* Čapek invented the word "robot" for his play, creating it from a Czech word that means "forced labor." The beings in the play that were created to serve humanity were living creatures, but the term "robot" was soon used in other speculative science fiction stories that featured artificial beings. Scientists and engineers who sought to develop machines that could help humans perform dangerous and tedious tasks also started using the word. It soon came to mean not just mechanical people made to serve humans but also any machine that's designed to carry out a series of tasks in the same way automatically.

The science fiction writer and biochemist Isaac Asimov coined the word "robotics" in 1941 to describe a scientific discipline that did not exist at that time. Asimov, whose stories contributed important ideas to the development of robots, didn't realize he was inventing a new word. He wanted a simple word

ROBOTS, JOBS, AND YOU

Jason Porterfield

Rosen
YA™

New York

Published in 2020 by The Rosen Publishing Group, Inc.
29 East 21st Street, New York, NY 10010

Library of Congress Cataloging-in-Publication Data

Names: Porterfield, Jason, author.
Title: Robots, jobs, and you / Jason Porterfield.
Description: First edition. | New York, NY: The Rosen Publishing Group, Inc., 2020. |
Series: The promise and perils of technology | Includes bibliographical references and
index. | Audience: Grades 7–12.
Identifiers: LCCN 2018046854 | ISBN 9781508188346 (library bound) |
ISBN 9781508188339 (pbk.)
Subjects: LCSH: Robots, Industrial—Juvenile literature. | Robotics—Social aspects—
Juvenile literature.
Classification: LCC TJ211.2 .P6725 2020 | DDC 338/.064—dc23
LC record available at https://lccn.loc.gov/2018046854

Manufactured in the United States of America

The early industrial robot Unimate performed delicate tasks, such as picking up an egg and pouring tea, during a 1967 demonstration.

that could encompass all the various branches of science that are involved in creating robots.

When the first factory robots were developed in the 1950s, they looked nothing like people. Instead, they were built to carry out specific tasks in the most efficient way possible. They could do many of the harder and more dangerous jobs in factories. The people who previously worked at those jobs could move on to other tasks. Robots have since been introduced to many different industries, where they have improved productivity.

There is a fear that robots are becoming too common and that they are taking over many people's jobs. Some industries such as mining and manufacturing have become heavily automated thanks to robots. In many cases, however, the presence of robots opens up new job opportunities for people with the right training. People with training in STEM (science, technology, engineering, and mathematics) fields, such as computer programming and electrical engineering, can expect to find many jobs that offer the chance to work with robots in these growing fields.

Creating Artificial Life

For thousands of years, people have imagined inanimate objects that can take on lives of their own. Various cultures have stories in which carved statues, puppets, or elaborate mechanical devices are created to handle certain tasks. In later years, engineers worked to create devices that could perform the work of human beings in an efficient way.

In the mythology of the ancient Greeks, the craftsman and inventor Daedalus built incredibly lifelike statues out of bronze in his workshop that moved in a lifelike way. They could even move their limbs and weep.

Daedalus also created Talos, a giant automated bronze warrior who protected the island of Crete from potential invaders. Talos specialized in throwing boulders at ships as they approached the island until the sorceress Medea convinced him to

In the 1963 film *Jason and the Argonauts*, the mythical bronze giant Talos tries to destroy the story's heroes before they manage to defeat him.

remove a plug from his body. The ichor (or fluid) that gave him life flowed out of his body, killing him.

Another figure from Greek mythology, Pygmalion, was a skilled artist. He sculpted a statue of a woman so beautiful that he fell in love with it. The statue, named Galatea, came to life through the intervention of the goddess Aphrodite. Galatea and Pygmalion married and had a family together.

Early Robots

Inanimate objects didn't come to life only in myths. Centuries ago, skilled artisans could create mechanical devices called automata that were designed to mimic living things. They were designed to entertain people, usually the wealthy patrons of the artisans who built them.

Mechanical automata might look like birds, animals, or people. Artisans and inventors powered them with springs, water, or forced air. Automata mechanisms moved in various ways. Some could even make music or dance.

Automata date back centuries in some cultures. The Turkish scientist and inventor Ismail al-Jazari and the French inventor Jacques de Vaucanson were among the best-known builders of automata. Al-Jazari lived during the twelfth and thirteenth centuries. His stunning works included hydraulic (water-powered) clocks, a mechanical orchestra that could make music, and a machine that served wine automatically. Many of his inventions were described in the book he wrote, *Book of Knowledge of Ingenious Mechanical Devices*.

Jacques de Vaucanson, who lived during the eighteenth century, invented complex automata, including mechanical musicians and a clever device called the Digesting Duck. Completed in 1739, this mechanical duck contained a system of rubber tubes and weights that could make it flap its wings and appear to eat and drink.

In the early twentieth century, new technologies such as widespread electrical networks and radio inspired new ways of

Inventor Jacques de Vaucanson's creations included lifelike automata in the form of a shepherd (*top right*) that could play several songs on the flute and a digesting duck (*top left*) that seemingly could eat and digest kernels

envisioning mechanical humans. People began considering the possibility of mechanical servants that could lessen their workloads. Several companies developed demonstration robots that could be controlled to mimic human actions. Devices such as Eric, Herbert Televox, and Elektro the Moto-Man could do things like stand up and "speak" through hidden record players. These demonstration robots amazed spectators, but they could not be programmed to act on their own.

Putting the Pieces Together

Technology made major strides throughout the first half of the twentieth century. Inventions such as the radio, automobiles, and the affordable means of producing and delivering electricity had opened up new possibilities. The early demonstration robots showed the public that new technologies could be harnessed in incredible ways.

More advanced technologies had to be developed before robots could be anything more than electric demonstration pieces or mechanical automata. The development of early computers helped lead the way for many of those changes.

Telephone technology was first used to build computers that could perform calculations in the early 1940s. In 1943, work began on the Electronic Numerical Integrator and Computer (ENIAC) computing system at the University of Pennsylvania, a project funded by the US Army. When it was completed in 1945 and made public by the army in 1946, it was among the first general-purpose computers ever built that was totally digital. ENIAC could perform calculations one thousand times faster than the electromechanical machines in use at the time, according to the 1946 *New York Times* ENIAC article posted on the website of the Computer History Museum.

Early computer operators who worked on ENIAC had to adjust switches and plug in and unplug cables so that the machine could perform its functions.

Early computers like ENIAC were enormous. They filled massive rooms and needed huge amounts of electricity to work. Engineers looked for ways to develop new computers that took up less space and required less energy. Improvements to electrical circuitry and radio technology gave researchers more tools to build increasingly more complex devices, which would in time be used to program robots.

While engineers were working on making computers smaller and more efficient, efforts were also underway to build practical robots. In 1948 and 1949, the Burden Neurological Institute in Bristol,

England, developed a pair of electric robots that could move on their own without outside controls.

Their inventor, W. Grey Walter, called them tortoises because of their size, shape, and the slow pace at which they moved. Walter built the tortoises, named Elmer and Elsie, to help study how the human brain worked. Walter wanted to demonstrate his theory that only a few brain cells could control complicated human thoughts and actions. The tortoises were made up of electric circuits inside a plastic shell. The shells contained sensors that could detect light and signal for the tortoises to move based on those signals. The shells also sensed when the tortoises bumped into another object, then signaled the devices to move in another direction.

The development of computers, small electric motors, and improved circuitry had made the tortoises possible. The tortoises

The Microchip

Microchips, sometimes called integrated circuits, are among the most important components inside computers and other sophisticated devices such as robots. They are small slices of silicon that contain thousands of tiny electronic components like transistors or capacitors. Microchips were developed in 1958 by Robert Noyce of Fairchild Semiconductor and Jack Kilby of Texas Instruments. They wanted to find a way to reduce the amount of energy computers and other electric devices needed. The tiny components on each microchip carry out the same processes that were once performed by larger mechanisms. The development of microchips made smaller computers and other devices a reality. Microchips have gotten increasingly smaller since 1958, allowing for more and more powerful machines to be built.

themselves showed that even simple electrical structures could move in complex ways. The tortoises also marked the first slow steps toward the development of artificial intelligence.

Other researchers and engineers began thinking about whether machines could also be made to "think," or perform functions that mimic human thought. John McCarthy, a mathematics professor and future computer science professor, coined the term "artificial intelligence." McCarthy was hosting a conference at Dartmouth College and wanted to describe how automated machines processed information. He believed that any type of instruction or information could be broken down into simple parts that a machine could understand. Artificial intelligence became one of the dominant ideas in robotics.

Robots Under Development

In 1954, inventor George Devol applied for a patent for a device called the Programmed Article Transfer. The device Devol envisioned was the world's first programmable robotic arm. Unlike the robots of science fiction or the demonstration robots built earlier in the twentieth century, the Programmed Article Transfer looked nothing like a human being. It featured a single arm sticking out from a control box. The arm could be programmed to move through a series of switches. It used hydraulics to grip, lift, and move objects. Devol envisioned it as a general-purpose robot that could save time and energy in factories.

In 1956, Devol met a corporate executive and engineer, Joe Engelberger, at a party and told him about his invention. Engelberger, who was a fan of science fiction, thought the device sounded like a robot. They formed a partnership and found funding for their project. They focused on the machine's ability to do work that was considered harmful to people.

In 1959, they installed the first prototype of their arm, which they had named Unimate, in a General Motors factory in Trenton, New Jersey. The robotic arm was used there to produce die-cast vehicle parts like door handles, a job previously performed by human workers under dangerous conditions. The Unimate prototype was a success. They formed a company called Unimation, Incorporated, in 1961. Unimation was the world's first robotics company and soon began filling orders for more Unimate arms. Automobile manufacturers in the United States and Japan began using them.

Unimate and other early robots lacked any kind of external sensors that would make them useful for refined tasks. Instead, they performed simple tasks that called for moving and placing materials. Later, engineers could add sensors and controls that made it possible to use robots for tasks such as grinding and welding.

Unimate and similar industrial robots could keep things moving on the factory floor, but a greater level of refinement would be needed for them to perform more complicated tasks. In 1962, engineers working at Rancho Los Amigos Hospital in California created a device called the Rancho Arm to help people who were disabled and being treated there.

The Rancho Arm was developed to move more like a human arm. It had six different joints that let the people working its controls grasp, pick up, and move items. The range of motion was much greater than that offered by Unimate.

Stanford University bought the arm from the hospital in 1963 with the intent of refining its design. Researchers at the university used it as a starting point to build a more complex arm that was fully controlled by a computer. The Stanford Arm was completed in 1969 and had six joints as well as "fingers" that could grasp items. Optical and contact sensors, not unlike those in the tortoises, enabled engineers to use the robotic arm to perform some close mechanical work. The sensors helped it manipulate parts correctly as it put them together.

From 1966 to 1972, the Stanford Research Institute (SRI) developed a wheeled robot that that could see, move around,

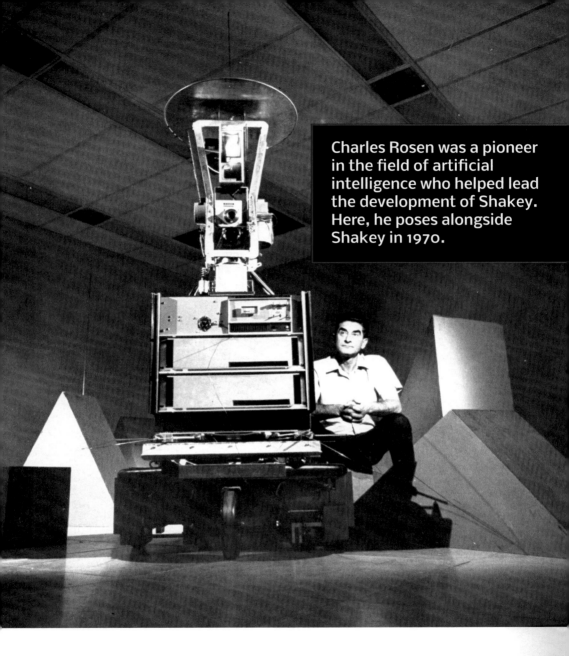

Charles Rosen was a pioneer in the field of artificial intelligence who helped lead the development of Shakey. Here, he poses alongside Shakey in 1970.

communicate, and touch objects. They called it Shakey for its awkward movements. Researchers used computer commands to control Shakey to perform tasks such as finding a particular object. The robot demonstrated the potential of artificial intelligence by calculating how to manipulate the object to complete its instructions.

The construction of Shakey later contributed to the invention of more sophisticated robot arms, spacecraft, and other automated devices.

Another robot arm called the Silver Arm was invented in 1974. It was designed to move like human hands. It could carry out precision assembly jobs and work with small parts. Japanese researchers working at Yamanashi University devised the Selective Compliance Assembly Robot Arm (SCARA) in 1978. It resembled the human arm in the way it moved, although its "wrist" joint was not made to tilt. When it was brought to factories in 1981, it demonstrated that it could move faster than other robot arms when picking up and placing objects. SCARA arms could also be built in different sizes, depending on the factory's need. These arms are found in factories all over the world, particularly where small electronics are manufactured.

Foundations of Robotics

The science of robotics requires an understanding of several different engineering and scientific disciplines. Electricity has been the key to building robots even from the first demonstration models built in the first half of the twentieth century. The people who built those contraptions and who have refined more practical robots over the years needed to be familiar with electrical engineering. They had to understand electrical circuitry, how power supplies work, how to regulate how much energy is used, and how to store energy for future use.

Computer science has been at the heart of most practical robotics applications since the development of Unimate. Computers are used to program robots. Computer hardware such as chips, microprocessors, and sensors for refined control are all necessary elements of robotics. Programmers provide robots with their instructions in code that signals components to move. Programming lets the robot know when to start, what to do in what order, and when to stop. Sensors enable the robots to carry out their tasks with precision.

Mechanical engineering is necessary for ensuring that the robot can move in the most efficient way possible. Mechanical engineers consider how joints work, how to maximize articulation, and how to connect motors and power sources. Mechanical engineers work out how to make robots strong enough and durable enough to perform their tasks over and over without wearing out or breaking down.

Materials science describes the discovery and development of new materials for building and manufacturing purposes. Materials science is important in designing robots that will hold up under heavy use. For robots to be useful, engineers have to choose durable materials for their construction. Materials science researchers consider metal alloys and different types of plastic for their robots, depending on their intended use.

The Factory Floor

Since the development of Unimate, robots have become a common presence in factories and manufacturing. They have led to increases in factory productivity, but have also helped bring about the loss of manufacturing jobs. Many of those jobs were once the most difficult, dangerous, and dull tasks factory workers had to perform. Often, factories are divided into areas where robots operate and places where human workers carry out their roles in keeping production moving along.

Factories remain the setting in which robots are most frequently used. Many manufacturers depend on the machines to do work more quickly and precisely than humans. A number of manufacturing industries have become dominated by robots. Factories where goods such as vehicles, appliances, and electronics in particular often have a sizable robot presence.

Robots on the Job

Manufacturing robots are generally modeled after several types. These basic types can be adapted to a wide range of different uses in a variety of settings. A person might find some of the same types of robots in a factory that makes toys that are in use in assembling vehicles. Most factory robots are variations on the common arm type inspired by Unimate and improved on through technological advances. SCARA robots remain common in factories around the world.

Articulated robots have an arm that's connected to an immobile base and at least two joints that connect each section of arm. One joint located at the base allows the arm to rotate. Each additional joint, called an axis, allows the arm to move in a given direction. Simple articulated robots may have just two joints. Others may have more than ten joints linking them together. In factory settings, most articulated robots have from four to six joints.

Delta robots have three arms that work from one base to move the end effector, which is the part of the robot that interacts with the material it is handling. Delta robots were first developed in the 1980s to work with small objects such as electronics components. They are often used for packaging and assembling objects with small pieces, such as medical devices. They are able to move quickly and precisely.

Gantry robots are designed to move only in straight lines. They can move up and down and from side to side through their three linear joints. They are very precise and easy to program. Gantry robots generally have an arm that's attached to an overhead structure that allows it to carry out its tasks from above. They are used in many ways, including pick-and-place jobs and welding. They might drill holes in a crowded automobile factory or move objects around in warehouses.

Polar robots, also called spherical robots, feature a base with a twisting joint. The arm itself has a pair of rotary joints that give it the freedom to move around in a circle and a linear joint to move it up and down.

Robots in the System

In many factory settings where robots are used, the machines are in one area performing their tasks, while the human employees are on the other side doing theirs. The separation of robots from human workers is due mostly to safety reasons. Robots are programmed to perform their tasks over and over, without pause. A careless human

The multiple controlling arms of this delta robot, called Sketchy by its builders, enable it to use a pen to draw shapes and portraits of people.

worker who accidentally gets in the way of a robot cannot expect it to stop moving. Robots in those parts of a factory, warehouse, or other workplace are programmed to run nonstop without interference from human workers. Unless they are taken off the line for maintenance work or repairs, they are always doing their jobs.

Robots are programmed to make precise movements without any variation. Manufactured parts—from vehicles to speakers—have to be made in exactly the right way to fit together correctly and to work properly, without causing problems for the user.

Industrial robots are usually programmed through a handheld device called a teach pendant, featuring a number of command buttons. The operator uses it to punch in the commands for the specific tasks the robot is supposed to perform. They may include the direction of movement, speed, and other variables, depending on how the robot is being used. Teach pendants can be either connected to an immobile part of the robot (such as the base) or they may be wireless. The programmed commands enable the robots to work together as part of an assembly line, each doing its job before the product or component being built moves along to the next robot.

Many robots found in factory settings are assembly line robots that perform tasks like welding, stamping, or drilling. They may turn or hold large components such as car doors, or fasten tiny components onto circuit boards. Some grind rough pieces to the level of smoothness needed for parts to fit together or to allow paint to be applied properly.

Packing robots specialize in placing materials in their proper packaging so that they can be shipped out to a warehouse before going out to consumers. Automatically guided vehicles (AGVs) are robot vehicles that are used to transport materials through factories. They are programmed to follow wires or other markers through the factory and to make stops when needed. Workers themselves don't have to take time to move components around, potentially delivering parts to the wrong place or causing an accident.

Teach pendants give factory workers the ability to program and control robots from a safe distance as they carry out difficult jobs, like moving heavy objects.

Robot Benefits

Robots hold several advantages over humans that are useful on the factory floor. Robots don't have the same physical limitations as people. Even the best workers need to take breaks. In the United States and many other nations, there are limits to the number of hours workers can stay on the job without a break. Even if the work is relatively easy, workers performing the same task over and over may get bored. Their concentration can slip, leading to mistakes. Robots, however, can maintain the pace their programming allows and can keep doing the same work quickly and efficiently.

Human employees also get sick. They may have to stay at home to recover from an illness, whether it's a bad cold or something much more serious. Workplace injuries are another worry for human

Soft Robotics

Industrial robots are generally made from metals such as steel that are designed to withstand years of heavy use. Their metal construction is one of the factors that makes them so dangerous for humans to work around. Engineers who work in the field of soft robotics study ways to make robots safer by using more flexible materials such as silicone.

These robots are much lighter than traditional assembly line robots and less likely to cause serious harm to human workers. Their softer materials make it easier for them to perform delicate tasks and manipulate items that might give traditional robots problems. Soft robotics machines are also designed to move in a more naturalistic way, giving them the ability to pick up and work with more delicate objects. Soft robotics robots are also developed for uses in health care fields.

employees that robots don't face. In factory settings, dangerous machines can seriously hurt or even kill workers. Conditions such as high temperatures or fumes can cause physical harm or at least discomfort. Robots might be damaged in an accident, but they won't be scarred for life or hurt so that they can't work. Damaged robots can always be fixed or replaced. Injuries to people can be permanent.

Robots can be used to handle dangerous materials at a safe distance from people. They may be programmed to destroy chemicals or weapons that can cause great harm.

Manufacturers also see robots as less expensive than human workers. Robots don't have to be paid a salary or an hourly wage. They also don't receive benefits such as health insurance. A factory that operates around the clock needs three shifts of employees working eight hours each to keep production moving. Manufacturing companies can reduce their workforce expenses by replacing those jobs with robots that can work all day and all night.

Human-Robot Conflicts

At first glance, it seems logical to make factories fully automated workplaces without human employees. However, there are several downsides to doing so, and many positive benefits human workers bring to factories.

Robots don't have to collect salaries, take time off, or receive benefits. That doesn't mean that they are inexpensive. Initially, robots are very costly. A robot arm with a teach pendant and programming included might cost its owners hundreds of thousands of dollars by the time it's set up and running. Industrial robots are built to last, but they still break down. Repairs and replacement parts can be costly, as can the routine maintenance needed to keep them going. Robots need to be inspected regularly to ensure that they are working properly and are safe to use.

Robots are limited by the fact that they can't perform tasks outside their programming. If changes are made to the assembly line, they may have to be reprogrammed so that they are performing their tasks correctly. A factory that changes the line of products it makes might have to reprogram most of its robots or even replace them.

Even though factories typically keep human workers and robots separated, accidents can occur. The United States Occupational Safety and Health Administration (OSHA) reported that there were thirty-nine robot-related accidents involving human workers between 1984 and September 2018. Twenty-seven of those accidents were fatal to the person involved. Others resulted in serious injuries. In many cases, the worker was pinned by the robot or struck by it as it performed its tasks. Unlike a human equipment operator, a robot can't be alerted when a worker gets caught in the machinery. The robot doesn't stop until someone shuts it down.

Robots also replace human workers, leading to job losses. Their presence in factory assembly lines and warehouses has meant fewer employment opportunities for human workers, particularly those without specialized skills or training. Even work once done by skilled machinists, such as drilling holes or welding, is often done by robots.

Working with Robots

In many cases, the industrial jobs robots have taken from people in factories are among the most repetitive, dangerous, or uncomfortable. Robots can do these jobs without the quality of their work slipping. Once robots are programmed and have been started, they can keep working without any input from humans.

Although many different kinds of robots have been developed since the first Unimate machines were built, there are some jobs that require human beings because they are beyond the abilities of robots. To run smoothly, factories need programmers who can enter the robots' commands and start the machines. Engineers work to set up the robots and develop systems that can maximize their productivity. They ensure that productivity goals are being met and make adjustments to the system as needed.

Maintenance workers make sure the factory's structure and internal systems are all in good shape so that the human employees and robots have a stable environment in which to work. Depending on their specialties, they may be asked to handle plumbing problems, wiring issues, or even repairs to the building itself. Custodians keep the factory clean so that debris and dirt don't interfere with workers or with robots.

Factories also have workers who specialize in quality control. These employees confirm that the products or components being produced meet rigorous standards. Robots don't have the ability to make such assessments.

STEM skills are needed to fill many of those jobs. Engineers and maintenance workers need to know how to read blueprints and integrate robots into the factory's systems. Programmers must be able to use the robot's programming language correctly. The quality control professionals will have to be able to make calculations and take measurements to make their assessments. Although robots have taken some skilled factory jobs, there is still a place for human workers in manufacturing. Engineers may develop robots in the future that can perform complex tasks such as quality control work, but capable technicians will still be needed to take care of them and make sure production is on track.

Reaching Scientific Horizons

There are limits to the conditions the human body can endure and to the places people can go without help from machines. Scientists who want to learn more about places like outer space, the deep sea, polar regions, and active volcanoes can use robots to help with their research. Robots can withstand environmental conditions that humans cannot survive. Their programming or the ability for scientists to control them remotely enables them to perform complex tasks with precision.

Many of these research tasks would be impossible for humans because of extreme external conditions, such as crushing oceanic pressure or a lack of breathable air. These scientific robots make it possible to learn more about the world.

The Earth's Extremes

Harsh environments make it difficult or impossible for humans to visit some places on Earth. Robots are used to gather data far out at sea or in ocean depths that humans can't survive on their own. They can gather data about phenomena that scientists are trying to understand, such as atmospheric changes.

Robots can be particularly useful in helping researchers gather information about the climate. Climate robots are relatively simple machines. They are designed to be positioned in places where it might be challenging or impossible for human beings to stay. They are programmed to collect and record data such as rainfall amounts

The NASA robot Zoe, shown in 2013, was designed to scout for signs of life in Chile's Atacama Desert as a way to prepare for future missions to Mars.

and temperatures over time. This information can be used by climate scientists to monitor changes and make predictions.

Climate robots might be placed in underwater environments, on mountaintops, in deserts, or at Earth's poles. They come in many different shapes. Like industrial robots, they do not resemble people at all. Aquatic robots used for measuring data such as water temperatures and currents have tapered, cylindrical bodies that make them look like torpedoes. They even have fins to stabilize them while they are in the water.

Engineers have worked on round robots that move across the land like tumbleweeds for use in deserts. These robots would gather data for scientists as they roll along. A solar-powered robot named Zoe is used to search for microorganisms in the extremely dry climate of the Atacama Desert of northern Chile.

Other robots serve the scientists who are working to gather data. In Antarctica, robotic rovers are used to detect crevasses in the ice that could prove to be dangerous to convoys. They also explore caves under the surface ice, gathering information about conditions in such hard-to-reach places.

Robots used in scientific research go to places human beings cannot easily visit. Instead of taking jobs away from human workers, they actually make many jobs possible. Researchers depend on the data gathered by these robots to develop new ideas or prove scientific theories. Jobs are created for support teams who provide assistance on scientific expeditions that use robots.

Reaching the Stars

Robots have played vital roles in humanity's efforts to learn more about outer space. Automated rovers and spacecraft that can perform tasks based on their programming give scientists access to parts of outer space that are too far away for astronauts to reach.

Unmanned space probes are robots that gather data, respond to commands sent from Earth, and transmit the information they

Volcanic Secrets

Toxic gases. Treacherous terrain. And, of course, boiling lava. It's challenging for human beings to get a close-up glimpse of an active volcano. For that reason, the process of how volcanoes erupt remains something of a mystery. Robots, however, can venture into passages too dangerous or simply too small for humans to explore. In 2014, a small wheeled robot called VolcanoBot 1 descended into an inactive fissure—a crack that spews molten rock called magma—in a Hawaiian volcano. Researchers were astonished to discover that the robot reached the end of its tether, descending 82 feet (25 meters) into the ground, without hitting bottom. An improved robot called VolcanoBot 2 continued the work of mapping the fissure.

VolcanoBot's successors could someday travel into space to explore active and inactive volcanoes on the moon, Mars, and distant moons such as Enceladus, which orbits Saturn. Little is known about the mechanisms of how faraway volcanoes erupt.

This robot, called Dante II, was sent into the crater of an active volcano in Alaska to take samples of gases and water found inside, as well as to record video.

collect back to scientists. They have been used to study Earth's moon, distant planets, and comets. National Aeronautics and Space Administration's (NASA's) *Pioneer* and *Voyager* probes began flying past planets such as Venus, Saturn, and Jupiter in the 1970s. The probes *Pioneer Venus I* and *II*, for example, mapped that planet's surface and captured images of its clouds. Probes have grown more sophisticated over time with new technology. NASA has even sent probes to collect samples from comets.

Some of NASA's most successful research efforts of the twenty-first century have been due to robotic vehicles called rovers that are designed to fly through space, land on a moon or planet, and collect data. The rovers *Spirit* and *Opportunity* landed on Mars in 2012 to study the planet, map the surface, and provide data. They sent back important evidence that Mars once had flowing water on its surface and information about its massive storms.

Robotic arms are frequently used on the International Space Station (ISS) and on manned shuttle missions. They can perform difficult tasks outside the spacecraft's sealed environment. Astronauts can safely operate these arms from within the spacecraft to make repairs or install new equipment.

Unmanned transports have been developed to help deliver supplies to the ISS. These privately developed spacecraft operate without pilots or a human crew. Instead, they are guided to their destination from Earth. Some of these spacecraft have been programmed to return to Earth after they dock at the station and their cargoes are offloaded.

NASA's Robonaut project is an effort to develop a robot that resembles a human for missions in space. Robonauts are dexterous humanoid robots that are made to be used alongside human astronauts. Their shape is designed to enable them to use the same tools as their human counterparts. Robonauts such as the human torso–shaped R2 model have been used on the ISS.

Rather than taking human jobs, robots actually contribute to jobs for people in the space exploration field. These jobs are found

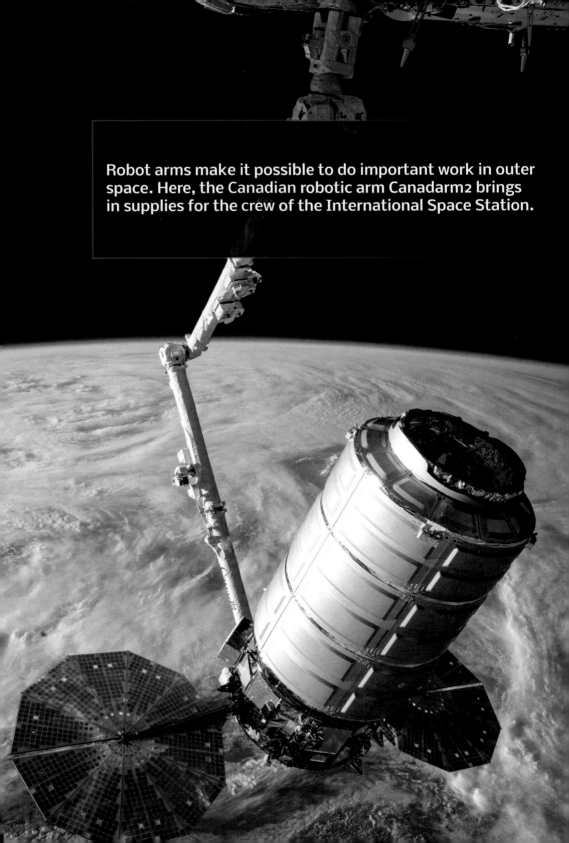

Robot arms make it possible to do important work in outer space. Here, the Canadian robotic arm Canadarm2 brings in supplies for the crew of the International Space Station.

in engineering, research and development of robots, and research in other fields. The information they contribute must be studied and analyzed by people. The robots themselves have to be designed, programmed, and repaired by skilled professionals. Although they are expensive, their cost is offset by the knowledge humanity can gain about the universe.

Robots and Health

There are many ways in which medical professionals can use robots to improve the quality of care and treatment for patients. Surgeons, pharmacists, and physical therapy specialists can use robots to benefit their patients.

Surgical robots are programmed to help doctors perform delicate operations. This procedure doesn't mean that hospitals turn patients over to robots to be operated on without any human oversight. Instead, surgeons use refined controls to manipulate the robots, which can remain steady and accurate enough to work on the brain, the heart, and other vital organs. Even the steadiest human hands holding instruments could cause irreversible harm in some of these surgeries.

Rehabilitation robots are used in patient recovery programs. They can help patients who have suffered strokes, undergone amputations, or experienced other traumatic medical events. While under the control of physical therapists, they might make it possible for people to recover functions like standing and walking.

Telemedicine robots are similar in some ways to surgical robots. They are used by doctors to check on how their patients are recovering. Doctors can control these robots by remote control and use video technology to communicate with their patients. They make it possible for doctors to give their patients high-quality care even if they are far away from one another. Telemedicine robots can be used in places such as rural areas where there is a shortage of

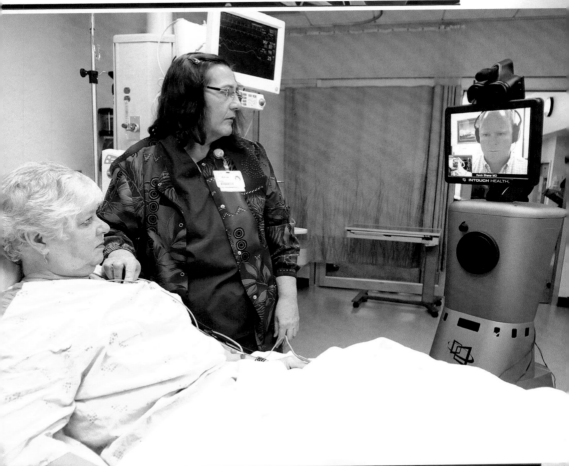

Telemedicine robots, such as the Robotic Office Diagnostic Assistant (RODA) machine, can help doctors communicate with and diagnose patients who are otherwise hard to reach.

doctors. They enable people to receive high-quality care that they wouldn't otherwise be able to access.

Robots can also help patients recover by providing medicine. Pharmacy robots are designed to give out prescription medication in precise doses. This technology can cut down on the possibility that a human pharmacist can make a potentially harmful mistake by incorrectly measuring out doses.

There are benefits and drawbacks to the use of robots in medical fields. Some robots, such as those used in pharmacies and rehabilitation facilities, directly take human jobs. However, robots can make up for a shortage of qualified medical professionals in rural areas and remote locations. They can also reduce the possibility of medical mistakes caused by human error. The future will bring more robots into medical settings with the development of a broader range of robotic tools with more advanced capabilities. In addition, the cost of such cutting-edge technology is likely to fall as the devices become widely adopted.

Dirty and Dangerous Jobs

Robots can be used effectively in jobs that are so physically demanding and so dangerous that few people want to do them. Other jobs might be beyond the abilities of people. In some cases, robots can be put to use in basic but dangerous tasks. The human workers they replace can then perform other jobs elsewhere that are just as critical.

Defense and Security

People are necessary for law enforcement, military jobs, and security tasks because they have the ability to make decisions quickly based on circumstances that may change rapidly. Robots can be used to perform some of the most tedious or dangerous tasks that humans are exposed to in those jobs. They also give professionals in these fields new tools they can use to protect people.

Some of the most visible military robots are drones. Military drones are most often used in places that are very difficult for human soldiers to reach. These aerial robots are designed to fly high in the air where they are difficult to spot from the ground. They are often guided by remote control from bases hundreds or even thousands of miles away and are programmed to carry out specific commands. From great heights they can carry out video surveillance missions. They take video footage of the ground so their operators can learn more about conditions in a certain area and see what potentially hostile forces are doing there.

Military drones give soldiers the ability to gather information about the terrain and enemy forces they'll face without having to put human scouts in danger.

Military drones are also used to attack specific targets. Their operators use video technology to identify these targets, including buildings, military installations, and even people. When the target is identified, the drone operator gives the command and the drone attacks with explosives.

Smart bombs are also used by the military to attack distant enemies from far away. They are explosives that are programmed to use global positioning coordinates to find specific targets after they are launched. If successful, these bombs can destroy their targets quickly without putting military personnel in danger. Unlike drones, they can be used only once.

Law enforcement agencies use drones for monitoring crowds and tracking suspected criminals. Like military drones, they can fly high above the ground and send real-time video footage back to their operators. They are commonly used by police departments in big cities to keep an eye on protests to make sure participants don't turn violent. Drones can follow people suspected of crimes from

Drone Debates

For military purposes, drones provide many advantages over manned aircraft. They require fewer personnel to operate them. They have a long range and are able to reach targets that may be inaccessible to manned aircraft. Most important, they reduce the risk to the operators—there's no pilot endangering his or her life in enemy territory.

The primary argument against military drones centers on civilian casualties—innocent victims killed or injured. Even when drone strikes by US forces are considered a military success, civilian casualties can potentially turn public opinion against American interests. In addition, there exists little international oversight of military drones. Drone warfare is likely to become more sophisticated. If hostile states or terrorists begin utilizing drones, the international community has no clear recourse for dealing with the situation.

above, passing over obstacles such as fences and over buildings that could slow officers on the ground.

Military and police agencies use specialized robots to defuse bombs. These sturdy robots can approach dangerous explosives without risking human lives. Video cameras allow their operators to see the bomb's wiring. They are operated by remote control to diffuse the explosives with their dexterous arms. Some sturdy robots are even designed to contain the explosives within themselves so that debris can't fly from the bomb and hurt people nearby.

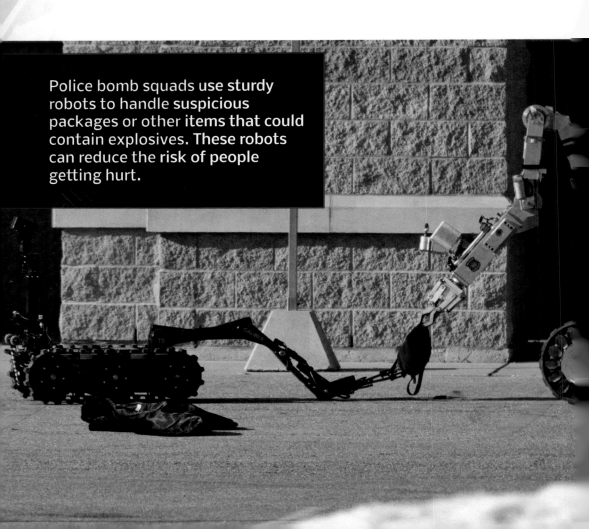

Police bomb squads use sturdy robots to handle suspicious packages or other items that could contain explosives. These robots can reduce the risk of people getting hurt.

Deep in the Mines

Mining is one of the most dangerous jobs in the world. Miners endure physically demanding work, hot conditions, exposure to deadly gases, and the danger of tunnel collapses. Even with modern technological tools, fatal mining accidents can happen. Many miners also suffer the aftereffects of injuries and exposure to harmful substances long after they stop working.

Industrial robots can be programmed to perform many of the most dangerous jobs in mining. They can carry out functions such as tunneling, removing rock, and bringing it up to safer levels for

processing. Such robots can perform their tasks under brutal conditions that are grueling for people to endure.

Mining robots are similar to robots found in factories. They can be programmed to do the same tasks over and over with precision. They do not resemble people in any way. Most look like automated versions of heavy equipment such as earth movers. Their programming instructs them where to go inside mines. Sensors tell them when to stop working and return to the surface.

Mining jobs have been disappearing steadily because of increased automation. It is cheaper and safer for mining companies to use robots in place of human workers. Mining robots don't tire like human workers. They can work steadily without stopping and cannot be

Mining robots make it possible to dig and take out natural resources, such as stones or metals, from deep underground that are otherwise difficult for people to reach safely.

injured. Improving technology will likely lead to an increase in the number of robots used in mining.

Fighting Fires

Firefighters risk their lives to put out burning buildings, vehicles, and wildfires. Some robots have been developed to handle several of their more dangerous tasks. Robots can endure the harsh conditions firefighters often face. Dangers such as smoke, extreme heat, and flames mean nothing to robots.

Human firefighters are trained to face many types of situations. They never know exactly what conditions they'll face until they arrive at the fire. Robotic firefighters are generally designed to perform particular jobs. They are built to sense fires, monitor their spread, and help put out flames. Firefighting robots are often sent into areas where conditions are too dangerous for their human counterparts.

Turbine-aided firefighting (TAF) robots are small vehicles that can be remotely operated to spray flames with water or foam. They can get close to flames and heat without being damaged. TAF machines have been used to put out factory fires in Europe and to fight wildfires in Australia.

Thermite robots are designed to enter wildfire areas. They are small vehicles that move along the ground on tank treads. They use cameras to relay video footage back to their operators, who can direct

Firefighting robots, such as this one spraying water on flames, are built to withstand the high temperatures and toxic fumes given off by fires.

them to spray water where it is most needed. Their rugged design gives them the ability to move over many types of terrain that might be difficult for human firefighters to navigate.

The Tactical Hazardous Operations Robot (THOR) is designed to enter structures that are on fire. These robots were originally developed by the US Navy to fight fires on ships. Unlike most robots, THOR machines are shaped like humans. These robots are equipped with cameras that give firefighters an idea of conditions inside. Their sensors make it possible for them to walk on unstable floors, open doors, and put out flames with water.

Firefighting robots have advantages and disadvantages. They can free human firefighters to work in less dangerous areas. They are rugged and difficult to damage. However, many have to be attached to a water supply to be effective. This requirement can limit their range. They also cannot react to changing situations like a human firefighter can. If a firefighting robot encounters a person in danger, it can't make the decision to stop spraying water to perform a rescue. These factors, along with high costs, make it unlikely that firefighting robots will replace their human counterparts. Instead, they will serve as useful tools in the important work of extinguishing fires.

Robots in People's Lives

Advances in robotics have led to many jobs being automated that were once carried out by human beings. In many cases, the machines can perform repetitive tasks quickly without making mistakes that workers might make. Jobs, especially entry-level positions, have been lost because of workers being replaced by robots in several industries such as banking and retail sales. Emerging technology will likely bring about even more changes in the future that will alter the way people work.

The Evolving Workforce

Robots have been developed to carry out basic, repetitive jobs. Many of the jobs they have taken are low paying and don't require much training. However, they also once gave employees a place to launch a career or at least earn some money.

Automated teller machines (ATMs) are unlikely to be the first devices that come to mind when people think of robots. These stationary machines are designed to give people quick access to money in their bank accounts. People with a bank card can use them to withdraw money, transfer funds, or see their account balance. They consist of a screen, number keys, a card reader, and slots for giving out cash and receipts.

The first ATM was installed in 1967 at a Barclays bank located in a suburb of London, England. The machines spread to the United States in 1969, when one was installed at a Chemical Bank branch

Automated teller machines (ATMs) have become such a common feature of everyday life that few people think of them as being robots.

in Rockville Centre, New York. Since then, thousands of ATMs have been installed in banks, stores, and restaurants. Many ATMs can be accessed after banks close, making them very convenient for people who need money right away. Automated banking is expected to contribute to job losses in the field, according to the US Bureau of Labor Statistics.

Automated checkout stations are beginning to replace human cashiers in stores. These devices scan the items the customer is buying, accept payments, give change, and issue receipts. They can even scan coupons. Grocery stores and big-box retailers such as Target use these checkout robotic devices. The online retailer Amazon has even begun opening stores called Amazon Go that automatically charge people for the items they're buying without making them go to any sort of checkout point. Customers just scan the Amazon Go app on their smartphone as they walk through a turnstile, shop, and then depart. These stores have a small group of human employees to keep shelves stocked and help customers. Amazon is planning to open thousands of these stores to serve workers who are too rushed to wait in line for the items they need.

Shoppers use their mobile devices to connect to their Amazon accounts and automatically pay for the products they purchase at an Amazon Go store in Seattle, Washington.

For decades, telephone companies relied on human operators to direct phone calls from one person to another through switchboards. Countless workers have been replaced by automated switchboards. Many other phone-oriented businesses that relied on humans to make and direct calls have also switched to robotic systems. These changes have a real impact on the number of people working in places such as call centers.

Transportation and Transit

Researchers continue to work on vehicles and mass transportation projects that can be programmed to get people to their destinations safely and efficiently. Self-driving cars are designed to do most of the work of driving. The cars have sensors that let them accelerate or slow down depending on traffic conditions. They can change lanes and respond to accidents ahead. Passengers simply enter their destination and the car either takes the route specified or one chosen by its Global Positioning System (GPS).

Self-driving cars have the potential to take jobs from professional drivers who work for taxi companies or ride-sharing services such as Uber or Lyft. The technology is also being adapted to be used in semitrucks used to ship goods across the country, as well as in buses and trains. Such changes can lead to job losses for operators, as well as job gains for engineers, programmers, and quality control specialists.

There are also concerns about the dangers posed by self-driving vehicles. They are designed to remove human error from the driving process. In theory, this feature should make them more efficient and safer. However, there is still a chance of fatal accidents occurring. The first such accident took place in May 2016, when an early self-driving car made by Tesla crashed into a truck. Investigators concluded that the driver and the car's computer both failed to see the truck because of bright driving conditions.

Drone technology is also being developed to deliver packages to people. Amazon and other companies that ship goods directly to customers have had some success with using drones to fly packages to homes. These developments could lead to job losses for delivery drivers, as well as for warehouse workers who pack delivery trucks.

Agricultural robots can be used to water plants and help farmers tend crops. This robot is detecting weeds for removal to make the growing process more efficient.

Robots at Home

Inventors and visionaries have dreamed of automated homes for decades. The idea that a person can have robot servants take care of their chores is appealing. Smartphones and wireless technology

Augmented Humans

Because of medical advances, there are already cyborgs — people with both biological and manufactured body parts — among humans. Modern-day cyborgs (from "cybernetic organisms") owe their health to devices and artificial components such as pacemakers and knee replacements. Technology can allow people who are deaf to hear through cochlear implants and restore movement to people who are paralyzed with a robotic exoskeleton.

There's nothing controversial about using devices such as prosthetics and implants for medical purposes. But in the future, people may be tempted to voluntarily modify themselves with high-tech augmentations. Devices or implants could improve physical or mental abilities. Brain-computer interfaces could someday connect people directly to their technological devices. It may sound far-fetched today, but rapidly evolving technology may eventually make such enhancements seem too good to resist.

have made home automation a reality for some people. Although the devices in an automated home don't look like the classic science fiction idea of a robot, they can be programmed according to the homeowner's preferences.

The internet of things (IoT) is a phrase that describes a network of interconnected devices that can communicate with one another. These connected networks are linked to a user's smartphone. The phone can then be used to program and control home systems such as thermostats, lighting, and security systems. "Smart" appliances like refrigerators can also be part of the network and controlled through smartphones. There are jobs in development, installation, and customer support.

People who have smart home systems can enjoy the convenience of using their mobile devices to turn on appliances, such as coffee makers, from far away.

The field of robotics has a bright future in many industries, although the outlook is mixed for some human workers. Many jobs have already been lost to robots in factories and mines. Other industries such as retail sales and banking could become heavily automated as robots become more common. In other areas such as medicine and scientific research, robots have filled valuable roles by performing tasks that are difficult or impossible for humans. Robots still need humans to function, and there will be places in the job market for people who are interested in robotics.

Glossary

artisan A person who is skilled in a particular art or trade.

assembly line A system of workers and machines in a factory working to assemble products in stages.

automaton (plural **automata**) A mostly self-operating mechanical device.

biochemist A scientist who works in biochemistry (the study of chemical processes that occur in living things).

circuit The path on which an electrical current flows.

component A part of a larger object, such as a vehicle.

dexterous Nimble and capable of a wide range of motion.

drone An unmanned aircraft that is controlled remotely by humans or navigates itself autonomously.

engineer Someone who designs or constructs engines or machines, or specializes in a branch such as electrical engineering or civil engineering.

fissure A crack or a split, particularly in Earth's surface.

hazardous Dangerous or risky.

humanoid Resembling a human being in appearance.

ichor A fluid, similar to blood, said to flow in the veins of the ancient Greek gods.

manipulate To control or handle in a skillful way.

mechanism A system of parts designed to work together.

microchip A series of electrical circuits contained within a small piece of silicon. Most electrical devices use microchips.

operator A person who controls or directs a machine or piece of equipment, including drones.

productivity The value of output compared with the value of input, especially in industry.

program To provide a computer or other device with encoded operating instructions.

rigorous Thorough and strict.

robot A machine capable of performing specific preprogrammed functions or tasks.

sensor A piece of equipment that monitors physical properties such as light or temperature.

surveillance Close observation or monitoring, such as of a particular site or group of people.

The Canada Science and Technology Museum

1867 St. Laurent Boulevard
Ottawa, ON K1G 5A3
Canada
(866) 442-4416
Website: https://ingeniumcanada.org
Facebook and Twitter: @SciTechMuseum
The Canada Science and Technology Museum features exhibits on Canada's achievements in science and technological innovation.

Computer History Museum

1401 North Shoreline Boulevard
Mountain View, CA 94043
(650) 810-1010
Website: http://www.computerhistory.org
Facebook: @computerhistory
Twitter: @ComputerHistory
The Computer History Museum explores the history of computing and its continued effect on society. It holds the largest global collection of computer artifacts in the world.

CyberneticZoo.com

Website: http://cyberneticzoo.com
The Cybernetic Zoo offers information and original source material about a wide range of robots, including pioneering machines and robots from science fiction.

National Aeronautics and Space Administration (NASA)

NASA Headquarters
300 E Street SW, Suite 5R30
Washington, DC 20546
(202) 358-0001
Website: https://www.nasa.gov
Facebook and Twitter: @NASA
NASA is a pioneer in developing and using robots for jobs that humans cannot perform.

National Sciences and Engineering Research Council–Canadian Field Robotics Network (NCFRN)

McGill University
James Administration Building
845 Sherbrooke Street West
Montreal, QC H3A 0G4
Canada
Website: http://ncfrn.mcgill.ca
The NCFRN brings together academic, government, and industry researchers to develop technology that enables robots to work together in outdoor environments.

The Robot Hall of Fame

Carnegie Mellon University
5000 Forbes Avenue
Pittsburgh, PA 15213
(412) 268-9752

Website: http://www.robothalloffame.org
Facebook and Twitter: @RobotHallofFame
The Robot Hall of Fame was created by Carnegie Mellon
University to recognize robot technology from around the world,
as well as robots from science fiction.

The Robotics Institute

Carnegie Mellon University
5000 Forbes Avenue
Pittsburgh PA 15213-3890
(412) 268-3818
Website: http://ri.cmu.edu
Facebook: @ri.cmu.edu
Twitter: @CMURobotics
The Robotics Institute at Carnegie Mellon University conducts
research in robotics technologies for use in industry and
society. It is committed to educating the next generation of
robotics engineers.

For Further Reading

Asimov, Isaac. *I, Robot*. New York, NY: Bantam Books, 2008.

Baum, Margaux. *The History of Robots and Robotics* (Hands-On Robotics). New York, NY: Rosen Publishing, 2018.

Cooper, James. *Inside Robotics* (The Geek's Guide to Computer Science). New York, NY: Rosen Publishing, 2019.

Jackson, Tom. *Will Robots Ever Be Smarter Than Humans? Theories About Artificial Intelligence* (Beyond the Theory: Science of the Future). New York, NY: Gareth Stevens Publishing, 2018.

La Bella, Laura. *The Future of Robotics* (Hands-On Robotics). New York, NY: Rosen Publishing, 2018.

Noll, Elizabeth. *Factory Robots* (World of Robots). Minnetonka, MN: Bellweather Media, 2017.

Peppas, Lynn. *Robotics* (Crabtree Chrome). New York, NY: Crabtree Publishing Company, 2015.

Porterfield, Jason. *Robots, Cyborgs, and Androids* (Sci-Fi or STEM?). New York, NY: Rosen Publishing, 2019.

Roberts, Dan. *Famous Robots and Cyborgs: An Encyclopedia of Robots from TV, Film, Literature, Comics, Toys, and More*. New York, NY: Skyhorse Publishing, 2014.

Ryan, Peter. *Powering Up a Career in Robotics* (Preparing for Tomorrow's Careers). New York, NY: Rosen Publishing, 2016.

Spilsbury, Louise. *Robotics* (Cutting-Edge Technology). New York, NY: Gareth Stevens Publishing, 2017.

Spilsbury, Louise. *Robots in Law Enforcement* (Amazing Robots). New York, NY: Gareth Stevens Publishing, 2016.

Bibliography

Allenby, Braden R., and Daniel Sarewitz. *The Techno-Human Condition*. Cambridge, MA: MIT Press, 2011.

Bailey, Diane E., and Paul M. Leonardi. *Technology Choices*. Cambridge, MA: MIT Press, 2015.

Computer History Museum. "Timeline of Computer History." Retrieved September 24, 2018. http://www.computerhistory .org/timeline/computers.

Edwards, Andrew V. *Digital Is Destroying Everything*. Lanham, MD: Rowman & Littlefield, 2015.

Favro, Terri. *Generation Robot*. New York, NY: Skyhorse Publishing, 2018.

Gabbert, Bill. "Firefighting Robots." *Wildfire Today*, December 11, 2015. https://wildfiretoday.com/2015/12/11/firefighting -robots.

Hobson, Rachel. "These Are the Robots You're Looking For." NASA, December 2, 2015. https://www.nasa.gov/mission _pages/station/research/news/robotics_in_space.

Kaplan, Jerry. *Humans Need Not Apply: A Guide to Wealth and Work in the Age of Artificial Intelligence*. New Haven, CT: Yale University Press, 2015.

Landau, Elizabeth. "NASA Robot Plunges into Volcano to Explore Fissure." NASA, January 7, 2015. https://www.nasa .gov/jpl/nasa-robot-plunges-into-volcano-to-explore-fissure.

Levy, Steven. "The Brief History of the ENIAC Computer." *Smithsonian Magazine*, November 2013. https://www .smithsonianmag.com/history/the-brief-history-of-the-eniac -computer-3889120.

McRobbie, Linda Rodriguez. "The ATM Is Dead: Long Live the ATM!" *Smithsonian Magazine*, January 8, 2015. https://www .smithsonianmag.com/history/atm-dead-long-live -atm-180953838.

Oskin, Becky. "Robot Called Yeti Finds Cracks in Antarctic Ice." *LiveScience*, March 5, 2013. https://www.livescience .com/27655-yeti-rover-antarctica.html.

Paterson, Euan. "Sea Robots Show Arctic Climate Change." Phys. org, June 8, 2018. https://phys.org/news/2018-06-sea-robots -arctic-climate.html.

RobotWorx. "Industrial Robot History." Retrieved November 20, 2018. https://www.robots.com/articles/industrial-robot -history.

Rosen, Rebecca A. "Unimate: The Story of George Devol and the First Robotic Arm." *Atlantic*, August 16, 2011. https://www .theatlantic.com/technology/archive/2011/08/unimate-the -story-of-george-devol-and-the-first-robotic-arm/243716.

Shewan, Dan. "Robots Will Destroy Our Jobs—and We're Not Ready for It." *Guardian*, January 11, 2017. https://www .theguardian.com/technology/2017/jan/11/robots-jobs -employees-artificial-intelligence.

Stewart, Jack. "Tesla's Autopilot Was Involved in Another Deadly Crash." *Wired*, March 30, 2018. https://www.wired.com/story /tesla-autopilot-self-driving-crash-california.

United States Department of Labor, *Occupational Outlook Handbook*, "Tellers." Retrieved September 21, 2018. https:// www.bls.gov/ooh/office-and-administrative-support/tellers .htm.

United States Department of Labor, Occupational Safety and Health Administration. "Accident Search Results—Robot." Retrieved September 22, 2018. **https://www.osha .gov/pls/imis/AccidentSearch.search?p_logger=1&acc _description=&acc_Abstract=&acc_keyword= robot&sic =&naics=&Office=All&officetype= All&endmonth =09&endday=19&endyear=1984&startmonth= 09&startday =19&startyear=2019&InspNr=.**

Wilkins, Johnathan. "Soft Robotics—The Future of Manufacturing Engineering?" *Engineers Journal*, May 9, 2017. http://www.engineersjournal.ie/2017/05/09/soft-robotics -manufacturing-industry.

Index

About the Author

Jason Porterfield is a writer, researcher, and journalist living in Chicago, Illinois. He frequently writes about tech and STEM-related subjects for young adults, including the books *Julian Assange and Wikileaks*; *Niklas Zennström and Skype*; *Angry Birds and Rovio Entertainment*; *Tim Berners-Lee*; *Conducting Basic and Advanced Searches*; *Aliens at Home: Studying Extreme Environment Species to Learn About Extraterrestrial Life*; *A Career as a Mobile App Developer*; and *Robots, Cyborgs, and Androids*.

Photo Credits

Design and Layout: Brian Garvey; Senior Editor: Kathy Kuhtz Campbell; Photo Researcher: Nicole DiMella